Bec Acopio is currently living in Maryland NSW with her son. She is writing fiction and non-fiction books for children and adults.

She is also writing books for relationships and spirituality. She divides her time between Newcastle and Sydney.

I Did Not Give Them My Consent

Bec L. Acopio

First published by Bec L. Acopio in 2017
This edition published in 2017 by Bec Acopio

Copyright © Bec L. Acopio 2017

The moral right of the author has been asserted.

All rights reserved. This publication (or any part of it) may not be reproduced or transmitted, copied, stored, distributed or otherwise made available by any person or entity (including Google, Amazon or similar organisations), in any form (electronic, digital, optical, mechanical) or by any means (photocopying, recording, scanning or otherwise) without prior written permission from the publisher.

I Did Not Give Them My Consent

EPUB format: 9781925579529
Print on Demand format: 9781925579536

Cover design by Red Tally Studios

Publishing services provided by Critical Mass
www.critmassconsulting.com

Contents

Acknowledgements vii

Chapter 1   1
Chapter 2   10
Chapter 3   20
Chapter 4   55
Chapter 5   60
Chapter 6   63
Chapter 7   66
Chapter 8   69
Chapter 9   71
Chapter 10   74
Chapter 11   78
Chapter 12   82
Chapter 13   85

Contents

Chapter 14 — 88
Chapter 15 — 92

Resources — 99

Acknowledgements

I'd like to thank God, the Divine Source within, my saviour, my mentor and my guidance. My Filipino family in heaven for their love and guidance. My children for their unconditional love, endless support and understanding. My nephews and their family for their love and prayers for me and for my children. Mr Marcelino Pajaroja and his wife Fernanda for their help and for being good friends as well as P. A. Brooker, Yolly F. and Estrella C. Shirley Atkin for helping me. G. Fischer, Literary scholar and historian, postgraduate degree (MA and PhD) in Comparative Literature from the State University of New York (Binghamton, NY), Adjunct professor of German and European studies at the University. Detective N. Web, from Belmont Police Station for taking my statement and trying to help me

Acknowledgements

out with my case.

Thank you to Maitland Member of Parliament MP, Jenny Aitchison, as the shadow minister for the prevention of domestic violence and sexual assault. Damon Cronshaw, NSW Newcastle Herald, journalist. NSW Health Education Centre Against Violence; for their Resources booklet, Recovering from Adult Sexual Assault.

Thank you too, to the following Medical professionals who helped me along with my healing journey: Jenny West, Accredited Mental Health Social Worker. Dr Cyriac Mathew, MD, FRAMZCP Clinical Director. Ben McIlroy, Brief Intervention Counsellor, Dip Couns. Cert. Trauma healing, Cert 1V Training & Assessment. Joan Gillis, Accredited Mental Health Social Worker (MSW, BSW, Ass. Dip. S. Wel., MAASW, Victims Services Counsellor. Dr Hashmi Shahid, GP. Chris Brown, psychologist, strengths based assessment and intervention. Liz Mullinar, A. M. B. Adv. Cert. in Trauma Healing, the CEO and Founder, of Heal for Life Foundation. Moira, Life line counsellor.

Anne Abbot, TAFE teacher. To all TAFE counsellors. John my Art teacher and his wife Hastings and to all my friends. Life line 24 hours phone counselling. NSW Government, Justice Victims Services. Safe houses & Human Resources. Especial thank you to Critical Mass Publishing, www.critmassconsulting.com.

Thank you all for everything.

Chapter 1

The Employer

Note: Names of all predators, places and other Filipino names were changed to protect individual's privacy.

I arrived in Australia around December 1989, it was before Christmas to be with my husband. I was 24 years old. In 1992 my husband found me a job from a local newspaper. I had no qualifications or skills at that time, so I had no choice but to take a job called a process worker, at one of the poultry factories in NSW. It was my very first job here in Australia. The work was terrible. The factory was very cold, noisy and smelly. Men and women had to do the same heavy lifting. I did not understand the language. The workers was swearing all the time, I had to ask the meaning of all the nasty words.

The factory employer, was called Roger. He was always smiling at me, every single day at work and, sometimes saying hi or hello. Maybe just being friendly or something, but I felt a bit uncomfortable especially if he talked to me very closely. Sometimes he would ask if I have family or relatives here in Australia and I'd say no, because they were all in the Philippines. The only family I had was my husband.

After three or four months working at the factory, my husband suggested for a divorce, because he noticed that I wasn't happy. I never smoke or drink alcohol in my life and, that's why I could not socialise with him and with his friends, almost every weekend. I've suggested to my husband to find me a place closer to my work, if possible and he did. Through Newcastle Star papers, he found me a place near my work. It was convenient for me, just 10minutes walk to the factory.

Nearly a year working at the factory, when one afternoon, it was five minutes before closing time. Roger came near me while I was working at the packing section. 'Hey Rebecca, could you go to my office for a minute?' Roger whispered in my right ear.

'Okay.' I replied. I was too shaky and nervous as I walked towards to his office, just one minute walk from where I was working. *I hope I'm not into trouble because I don't want to lose my only job*, I said to myself. I knocked on the door of his office.

Roger opened the door and let me in. He led me inside with a smiley face. He shut the door behind him. I nervously asked what I've done? He said, nothing. He opened a little fridge that was at the end corner of his little office. He took out of two dim sims and a can of coke. He opened the can before handing it to me and handing me two dim sims as well. We were just standing inside of his office not far from the door. He was too close nearly invading my private space, I moved backwards a bit and stopped against the wall.

'I have some instructions for you,' he said. He was going to say more but there was a knock on the door, so he moved backwards and opens the door. A male worker said something to him, I didn't know what it was, because I didn't hear it. I've heard Roger told the male worker to go back to his job, because he was busy at that moment. Then Roger closed the door, he came back to where I was standing. 'I want you to meet me up, at the bus stop near from your house, at exactly seven o'clock tonight,' Roger instructed me. 'Wait there for me and don't be late.'

I said, 'okay boss.' I was going to ask him why, but he told me to go back to my work. By the time I got back to my work station, the leading hand said to me that I could go home, work was finished for today. I went to the locker room, got changed and walked home as normal. My thought was filled with confusions and weirdness; why would the employer wanted to meet me, outside of working hours?

When I got home, I could not eat, I was still confused and feeling worried. *Why on earth the employer wanted to meet me?* I kept on saying to myself. I needed to get ready, because the boss told me not to be late and I don't want to get into trouble. I was feeling scared and at the same time some weird feelings in my stomach. I was thinking if I don't do what the boss said, he may sack me. If he sacked me, I won't be able to support myself as I have no family in Australia, besides I have no skills and qualifications to look for another job and I am only new in this country. I was baffled about what my boss's instructions. My mind was confused and scared, while I was walking towards the bus stop.

At exactly seven o'clock at night, I was standing at the bus stop, as instructed by my boss. Next minute, a Red Holden Commodore car stopped in front of me. It was the boss, Roger's car. Roger opened the front passenger's door by extending his hands to reached it. 'Get inside!' He commanded me. I didn't get in straight away as I was hesitant, feeling nervous and confused.

'GET IN QUICK!!' He yelled out. So, I forced myself to get inside his car, I was feeling uncomfortable sitting at the front. I could not say anything as I was feeling shaky and weird in my stomach. Somehow, I said to him something like... 'Where are you taking me?' I was feeling sick and too nervous and was hoping for him not to get angry at me by asking questions.

'I am taking you for a drive,' Roger said. Then he drove off. It was only about five or under ten minutes driving on the road, then he turned right into the dark place. There were lots of trees, there was no house not even one, just big and tall trees. The lights from the moon and stars, from the sky was the only lights on the creepy bush land. Roger parked the car. 'I found this place earlier before I picked you up.' He said. He got out from the car and went into the back seat. I was feeling scared for my life.

Roger instructed me again, 'Get out and sit here beside me.' I do as I'm told, because I don't want him to get angry at me, he was my boss at work. In my mind came the thought of; one of the Filipino cultures was, the workers must obey their boss. I was too scared, afraid and helpless; that if I don't do what the boss asks me to do, I'll get fired or sacked from work. At that moment, I just did whatever the boss instructed me. When I was getting inside the car at the back seat, my long hair got caught and stuck with something, I was trying to untangle it. So, it was taking me a bit to get inside. 'What's going on!! What are you doing? Roger, was getting annoyed. 'Why it's taking you too long to get in?' 'My hair is caught of something sharp and I don't know what this is.' I answered.

'Ah, that's my fishing rod. I told my wife, that I am going out to fishing tonight. Just hurry up!!' Roger demanded. He helped me untangled my hair out from his fishing rod. Then he grabbed my left hand roughly so I could get inside the car.

As soon as I got inside his car… 'Take your pants and undies off and hurry up!!' He said in a louder voice. In my mind came about the Philippine cultures; the workers or employees has no right to refuse any request/s or suggestion/s from their boss or employers, otherwise they will get fired or sacked; it was always yes boss was the right answer. I did not expect to be in this situation, my precious life was in a deep shit and petrified. I still want to live.

I was shaking nervously and confused, but I could not say a word. In my mind was asking why on earth my boss is doing this to me? This is not part of my job. But he was my boss at work, he's got the power and he is a big solid man. I just froze. I wanted to scream but there's no use, no one will hear me anyway, as we were in the middle of the thick bush.

'Do what I tell you to do if you want to keep your job!' Roger was getting impatient and yelled at me. He was using his power as an employer, to have the full control over me. At that moment; I was really petrified. I don't want to fight with him because he was a big man. I was too scared and afraid. He could kill me on the spot and, there will be no witnesses. If he kills me, he could just dump my body there. I still want to see my family overseas especially my Mum. I had no choice and no option at all at that very moment. He was my boss at work and in control over me. I just obeyed my boss; it was my survival.

As I was taking my pants off, his hands were all over touching my body; boobs, bottom and my private parts. I wanted to slap and spit on his f*ing face but I was powerless and hopeless. My boss, Roger grabbed my hips with his two hands and put me on his lap. He had no undies on, he raped me, sexually assaulted me at the back seat of his car. I could not do anything. My mind went elsewhere... my eyes were just filled with tears and I just succumbed... I still wanted to see my family overseas, if I scream for help no one will hear me anyway. I was surrendering myself from fear, being pressured, my job and my life, and was hoping he wouldn't kill me on that night. Because I still wanted to live for my family.

When he finally finished, he handed me a box of tissues. 'Wipe yourself up and get ready, I'll be dropping you home!! Just throw the used tissues outside the window!!' he commanded me again, while he was cleaning himself with the tissues. Then he told me to get out from his car and get back at the front passenger seat again. He also went back to his driver's seat at the front. I could not say anything, I was just feeling so scared for my life. 'Don't tell anybody or anyone, because it's a secret, understand? You don't want to end up losing your job and get into trouble!' My boss, Roger explained it very clearly.

I said to him, 'Okay.' I was just shivering, upset and very angry. He dropped me back off at the bus stop.

When I got home, I went straight to the bathroom, to clean myself up. I was just sitting there in the bathtub; feeling numb, emotionally and physically hurt and broken. At least I was still alive. I was still shaking, feeling sick and traumatised. I have lots of questions; why these was happening to me? Why the boss took advantage at me? Is it because I was vulnerable, alone and new in this country? And, don't know anything about the Australian law, women's rights and their system? Is it because I was an Asian girl, had no family and relatives to support me? Why? But I am also a human being; I have feelings too, I felt really hurt and broken. Too far different from the Embassy's information sessions; as the staff was showing us (people who were about to depart Philippines for Australia), and describing about all Australians were kind and caring people. The boss, Roger was the opposite, he was an Australian f*ing rapist man with no kindness at all. He was selfish, don't care about human being, he was a f*ing asshole.

It was a torture for me each time I went to work. One of the cultures in the Philippines is to keep quiet. Because rapes or sexual assaults were not being mention or talked about, it's too embarrassing to tell someone that, you're a victim of rape. So, I didn't tell anyone or anybody. I had nightmares and suffered depression and anxieties. I didn't tell my family overseas, because I didn't want them to get worried about me. I didn't want my Mum have a heart attack because of me. So, I just kept it to myself, I thought I could cope and just suffered in silence.

After a year working at the factory, I had shoulder and arm injuries, the company put me on light duties and terminated me after another year. There were many of us workers that had suffered work related injuries, because of the heavy lifting and repetitive work.

Chapter 2
The Pretender

My first day in Australia was in December 1989 to be with my first husband. In 1990, I've meet a Filipino woman called Daisy, at one of the gatherings at Hamilton Migrant Resource Centre (MRC), in NSW. She was working at this centre as a social worker for Filipino people. Daisy was nice, she told me if there's something I needed for help, just ring her up. In 1992, my first husband requested for a divorce. So, I've asked some help from Daisy. At that time, I was still working at the poultry factory in NSW, here in Australia and still living near my job. I paid Daisy $350 for helping and escorting me to the solicitor. Daisy offered if it was okay for me to be her adopted younger sister, because she knew, I had no family and relatives in Australia. So, I agreed with her and, I thought that it was nice of her.

worried maybe it will cause chaos and trouble. Besides, Barry told me not to tell his wife, because it will upset her deeply. He f*ing shouldn't have done it for the first place.

One day I was sorting out my photos because, I was thinking to send some of it overseas, for my family. Barry came over at my place alone again. I let him in, as a sign of respect; he was Daisy's husband. Besides, he won't do anything silly, because the owner of the house was at home too. Barry said that, he was on the way to work and, just dropping by because he bought something, as a surprise for me. He asked me what I was doing? I said I was sorting out all my photographs, because, I wanted to send some of it, over to my family in the Philippines. He saw my scattered photos on the floor. Then he looked at me.

'If you ever need to get your film printed or process, with some private or naked photos, and, you are feeling embarrassed to take it to the processing place, just ring me up. And I'll do it for you. I will post your film to the company and I will pay everything for you; including postage and processing,' Barry offered. I thought that's very strange offerings, why would he pay for my photographs? I could not say anything. I felt awkward and annoyed. I was trying to ignore him.

Barry took something out, from a David Jones black and white plastic bag. He showed it to me, by holding it up with his two hands. It was a matching pair set of bright, red silky lingerie. My eyes almost popped out, I was feeling confused again, how this man giving me such kinky stuff? 'You should be giving that to your wife, not to me.' I advised him and feeling a bit awkward.

'Daisy has plenty of these,' Barry said. 'Why don't you try these on?' Handing me the set of underwear, leaning forward to get closer to me. He was too close and invading my private space. I felt annoyed and uncomfortable. I moved backwards.

'Oh, No, sorry. I can't accept this. I am too embarrassed and feeling uncomfortable. I think this is not right. Sorry. I can't accept this, it's too much for me.' I handed it back to him. There was a silence of awkwardness, I felt threatened and scared again. I stared on the floor, I was hoping for him to go soon. I wanted to tell him to go, but I could not say it.

'No, don't be. I'm giving you these just a present, because you are my family now, remember?' He said, and refused to take it. 'What's your landlord's shift this week, is it day or night shift?'

'I'm not sure, but, lately he has been coming home in the morning. So, I think he is on night shift.' I replied. And then Barry left. He didn't take with him the set of underwear. I was still confused. For me, it was very weird to receive a gift of underwear, especially, from a married man and most all, he was my friend's husband. I thought, what the f*ck. I put the underwear on the very last drawer of my dressing table. I mean, seriously... I had no plan to wear it, just too awkward to think about it. I continued sorting my photographs.

The following night, around nine o'clock, when I was just got in bed there were knocks on the door, I opened the wooden door leaving the fly screen door still locked. It was Barry, he demanded to open the door for him. I've asked him what's going? Where's Daisy?

He said that Daisy was not with him. I thought maybe there's something wrong, maybe his car had broken down. He told me to open the door because it was an emergency, with louder demanding voices. I was shaking in opening the door. I was confused why on earth he dropped by unexpectedly at this hour, alone? *What's the emergency thing he was talking about? Was it about his family? I hope Daisy is alright.* I thought.

As soon as he was inside the house, he grabbed my arm tightly and almost dragging me into my bedroom. I was too scared with his strange actions, he has monsters' red eyes and telling me of what to do. 'Take your clothes off! It's payback time lady! There's no such things as free lunches anymore: The return trips to Sydney, weekend churches and gifts!' He said aggressively.

I was petrified for my life again. If I fight with him, he might kill me on that moment and, there would be no witness. I still wanted to see my family overseas, so I just obeyed what he tells me. He went on top of me, and sexually assaulted me in my own bedroom. I just closed my teary eyes, thinking for my family overseas. After he did it, 'I will tell Daisy all of it.' I declared.

'Oh, really? Do you think she will believe you? No one and nobody will ever believe you, take that in your mind. Stupid girl.' Then he left. Is that what a family member did to his family? I thought that, I could trust them as my family. F* you Barry and go to hell; another f*ing selfish Australian f*ing asshole. I felt really sick, I blamed myself for letting the predator inside the house. I just wished that I could be dead on that moment, but I still want to see my family. Barry took advantage of me, because I was vulnerable and had no family and relatives in this country. I just suffered in silence on top of everything.

On the following weekend Daisy rang me up as normal; she reminded me to get ready for church. But this time I refused to go to the church with them, I made excuses, I lied that I wasn't feeling well. I didn't feel comfortable anymore going to the church or going to their place and anywhere with them. I did not feel safe anymore and, I didn't want to get involved with the church anymore. I was going to tell Daisy about what Barry did to me and everything, but I was too worried, ashamed and scared. Daisy was fragile and dying and I love her so much as my sister. She was a lovely person; her husband was a monster. I didn't want to hurt Daisy's feelings, it's her f*ing husband's greediness and selfishness, that's why I kept away from them. After two weeks, Daisy died from breast cancer. I still went to her funeral to pay respect, for her kindness, love and care for me. Rest in peace Daisy, I love you my friend may your soul will go to heaven and I appreciate your kindness and everything you've done to me. While for Barry, he can go to hell and rot.

Chapter 3

The Landlord

I arrived my first day in Australia around December 1989 to be with my first husband and I was 24 years old. In 1992, my husband suggested for a divorce for some reasons. At that time, I was still working as a process worker at one of the poultry factories in NSW. My husband knew that I had no knowledge in getting around as I was only new in this country and hadn't travelled by public transport. So, he tried his very best to helped me find a place near my job. He did found one, it was advertised from the local Star Newspapers.

My husband took me at the new place, that had been advertised. The rent was $50 per week for a room and the food was not included of course. The owner of the house was called Preston. He said that he was a divorced man living by himself and was working at that time at BHP. According to him, he advertised one of his rooms for rent; to have an extra income and, so that someone will clean his house too.

The location was perfect and convenient for me, because it was only ten minutes walking distance to work. My husband had to explained to Preston about our separation things. I moved in at Preston's house on that same day. On my very first day, I've requested to Preston to put a padlock on my bedroom door. Preston said that he was a good person and I could trust him. But I still demanding to have a padlock on my bedroom just for my personal privacy. He did that and, he gave me two keys. Preston showed me where to buy my own food at the nearest Bilo grocery store, just 15 minutes walked from his house. Preston was a heavy smoker and, I've requested if it was okay with him; to smoke his cigarettes outside the house because, I can't stand the smell of it. Luckily, he agreed.

During my first three weeks living and renting at Preston's house, he would question me if I had family and relatives in this country. Even though, my husband has already told him that I had no family or relatives here. Otherwise, if I had, I would not need to be renting in one of his rooms. Anyway, I answered him that all my family and relatives were over in the Philippines.

After one month living or renting in his house, it was one afternoon. I was at the kitchen area, just doing the dishes. Preston suggested to stop doing the dishes, because he wanted to have a chat with me. He sat me down on the brown sofa near the kitchen. While he was sitting down on the floor and facing me.

'Rebecca, would you like to go out with me?' Preston asked the question. His eyes staring at me. I had no idea what he was talking about. So, I wanted to clarify it from him.

'Excuse me, I don't know what you mean, to go out with you, I do not know what you mean by that.' I asked him back. Squeezing my own hands and feeling a bit confused.

'What I mean was, would you like to be my girlfriend?' He said. 'Well...' He was waiting for my answer and his eyes staring at me.

What? He wanted me to be his girlfriend? What the... I was shocked! I took some deep breaths. My throat was tightening, almost chocking and grasping for some fresh air. I needed some help from my family for comfort or something and guidance.

'No.' I answered him firmly. 'As I am still feeling sad and hurt, from my separations with my husband,' I said to him. 'I am not ready yet for a new relationship. Besides you are too old for me and not my type sort of a man, if I was to look for one.'

'I'm only 13 years older than you and nothing wrong with that,' Preston said. His eyes still on me, he was touching and scratching his face and his balding head.

'No, thank you. Because legally; I am still married. I am not divorced yet, you know that, don't you? And, besides, I am not interested.' I felt disgusted, I excused myself and stood up, went back to finished my dishes and went to my room afterwards.

I was really annoyed by his proposal. I didn't want to be his girlfriend, no way. He had lots of grey hairs, wrinkled face, looking old enough to be my father and, a stinky heavy smoker. He looked like over 30 years older than me, no thanks, I am not interested. I don't think I would be his girlfriend ever. F*ck that, hopefully he won't ask me questions like that again.

One afternoon, when I got home from work, I went for a shower as usual. As I was getting an underwear, I've notice that my top drawer with underwear inside, was in a mess. I mean, all my underwear was always folded neatly, the way I liked it. But on that day, it wasn't folded anymore. It looked like, someone went through with it, searching for something. I thought it's weird, but I just ignored it. I was too tired from work. I believed that no one could ever enter my room, while I'm out because, it's locked each time I left for work.

Another afternoon when I went home from work, my garbage bin was in a big mess; my used sanity napkins were open, some bits and pieces was on the floor. I was angry and upset; I've finally had the courage to confront the owner of the house, Preston. I've asked and spoken to him, if someone had been into my room, while I was out? 'Excuse me Preston, did you go inside my room?' I asked him. 'because I've noticed my garbage bin…'

'Yes,' Preston answered. 'I had a spare key to your padlock, so I could get in and out to your room. This is my house, I can do whatever I like and no one can stop me. Not even you!'

'What?' I was pissed off. 'But why, Preston? Where's my privacy? I mean, what's the use of locking my room?' I felt really upset, but I could not argue for more, because I didn't want him to get angry at me. He may hurt or kill me. So, I just let it go.

'I went through your garbage bin, looking for some evidence like love letters or condoms etc. Because I wanted to know if you are seeing someone else and, I wanted to know if you have a boyfriend.'

'Preston!' I was feeling shitty. 'I mean, even if I had a boyfriend, seriously… it's not your business. I am not your wife, or girlfriend, or partner.' He had no right to know everything about me and he has no right to enter my room without my permission. I paid my rent for my room, so I had my rightful place for privacy.

I was furious and felt violated, the fact that he was breaching and disrespected my very own privacy. I was really upset and very angry, I paid my $50 weekly rent on time, I didn't understand at all…argh.

'Why, I have no privacy in this house? I pay my weekly rent on time, clean your house and I bought my own food. All I wanted is to have my own privacy. That's why I've requested a padlock to put on my door.'

'Remember, this is my bloody house, I still own the room and that I can do whatever I want!! And you are only renting a room as a tenant. SO, SHUT UP!!!'

I could not argue with him, he was right of course it was his house. Besides if I fight with him, maybe he will kick me out from his house and, if he did… I wouldn't know where to go. I can't fight with him, I was too scared and in fear, maybe he will kill me and I still wanted to see my family overseas. So, I just cope with it and let it go.

'Sorry, Rebecca. I won't go through your bin again.' He apologised. I could feel my face was burning and boiling with anger. If my anger looks could kill at someone, he could have been dead at that very moment. There's no use for me to argue with him, because I had nowhere else to go to. I didn't want to go back to my husband's house, because we were in a process of separations. F*you Preston, you are a sick psychopath. I just had to suffer in silence. It was like, I was in a jail or prison; with the doors open, but I could not leave, because I didn't know where else to go.

One afternoon during weekend, I was lying in bed and reading a book. I was in a big shock when Preston entered inside my room. What the f*ck…he had no clothes on, he was totally naked. My room has no lock from inside. It was so shocking and disgusting at the sight of him.

'SSSShhh…' putting his finger onto his lips… meaning shut up. 'Get your gear off!' He commanded, and gesturing waving his fingers at the same.

I'd freeze. I could not move… I was too scared that if I fight with him, he could have killed me on that moment and there will be no witness. I still wanted to live because, I still want to see my family overseas especially my Mum.

'Just do it!' Preston pressured me. I was petrified like a kid. So, I just obeyed and did what he wanted me to do. I took my pants off… Preston climbed on top of me and raped me… He sexually assaulted me. I could smell his awful cigarette breathe, his body and hands smelling cigarette too. I was really scared. I had no choice, but to kept quiet, because I still wanted to live. When he was finished…

'Zip locked your mouth, from now on,' He said. He went outside my room. I curled like a ball at the corner of my bed, crying, shaking and feeling so scared. I wished my Mum would be there beside me to comfort me and to get me out of that place. But I was alone and vulnerable.

After that day, he would come into my bedroom and raped me for at least once a week. I was Preston's sex slave, he told me to shut up if I say something. Sometimes he would take me to his bedroom too. He was so cruel. I wanted to kill myself, but I was worried my Mum will have a heart attack, so I just suffered in silence. I paid my $50 weekly rent, cleaned his house and bought my own food, why he wasn't still not satisfied? This landlord is a nut case predator. I wanted to move out, but I didn't know where else to go.

At that time, I was new in this country. I didn't know where to get some help, I had no idea if there were resources for women out there. I didn't tell anyone or anybody, maybe no one will ever believe me. Besides, where I came from, in the Philippines, it was too embarrassing to discuss about rape or sexual assaults. No one or nobody wanted to know about this topic or subject about sexual assault things. I've learned to accept it that this was my life, I had to dealt and cope with it. I was just kept on hoping and praying that, one day I will be strong enough to move out and have a place to live into.

I've joined the Gym nearby, it was 15minutes walking distance from Preston's house, just to get away from him. Sometimes Preston would question me each time I get home from the Gym, with his hands on my arms; shaking me like a kid and saying, 'look at me in my eyes and tell me where have you been!!' Even if I told him where I went, most of the times he wouldn't believe me and would get angry at me. I was living in fear, powerless, I could not fight with him and I was too scared maybe he will kill me. He treated me like a piece of thing, he thought that he owned me. I had to be brave and strong for my family. I just had to put up with him, because I didn't know where else to go.

One afternoon my Filipino workmate, Mia, invited and picked me up from my place. It was her birthday party at her place at Edgeworth. After the party, it was already night time. One of Mia's male friend offered to drop me off, because she was very tired. As the car approaching slowly and pulling over at my place, I spotted Preston hiding behind the shrub bushes at his front lawn. No one could miss his head sticking out, because he was six feet four and taller than the trimmed shrub. I thought, *what the f*ck was he doing there, standing like a statue or a creepy spy?*

When I got out from the car, Preston followed behind me until we get inside his house. I was going to go straight to my bedroom, but he stopped me by holding my left arm. I was terrified that he may hurt me or something. Preston has had unpredictable behaviours and attitudes. He could be aggressive at any time. Many occasions that he would just stared at me at the kitchen, while I was doing the dishes, or he would question me badly like I was his own property. A controlling psychopathic nick name? would really and absolutely fit for him. That evening, he stopped me from going straight to my room.

'I saw you with a man, who was he?' He questioned me like a kid, holding my both arms. His eyes were turning red like an angry monster, staring at me. 'Look me in the eyes and answer me, who was that man who dropped you off?'

'And I saw you too, behind the shrub bushes.' I said, feeling really scared. 'The man was Mia's friend.' Why I had to explained to him where I've been and why he is worse than my father? I was hoping he wouldn't hurt me. I wanted to slap his face but I was feeling hopeless.

'I could not find you anywhere around the house. I'd been going back and forth from the garage, around the backyard and around the front yard for over three hours,' He continued. 'I consumed a packet of cigarettes and that, it's all your fault for not letting me know. You should ask or at least tell me your daily activities things. It's my house rules and regulations, you must follow it.'

'And, why should I?' F*ing twisted mind. In my opinion, he had no right to know everything I do.

This is ridiculous. I am an adult person and I am not in a relationship with him. Why he is treating me like a kid or a shit?

'You must inform me, every single thing and, before doing something specially if going outside my house. I wanted to know what, where, why and when will you be home. This is my house, remember?' Preston declared it to me very clearly.

I could not comprehend in my mind; why he would be wanting to know everything and everywhere I go? I mean, hey I am only his tenant, yes, he was sexually abusing me now and then and, over powering me, because I was helpless, vulnerable and didn't have a place to go to. But I wasn't his partner or his property thing. What was his problem, why he was madding at me? Any way I could not argue with him, because it'll make things worse.

He questioned me where I've been and who I was with for the whole night. He asked me if I had sex with the man. I told him that it's not his business because I wasn't in a relationship with him. He got really mad and yelled at me forcing me to tell him everything. At that moment, it was ridiculous, absurd; there's no point and I could not argue with him, I think, this man is a freak damn nut case. So, I had to tell him forcefully, that it was Mia's birthday party. He did not believe me anyway, because it wasn't Mia who drop me home. As usual he nagged at me with his loud voices for not asking his permission before going out and that he branded me as a naughty girl and for being a bad girl.

I would like to say, he was worse than my biological parents. As I did not ever experience some sort of cruelties, or controlling badly like Preston. My upbringing from my parents, was lovely, they looked after me; with unconditional love and care and the right discipline for a human being.

I was getting used to at Preston's bad behaviours, unpredictable mood swings, controlling and sexual assaults. I had accepted it all in my head, that I was living with this crazy predator; the pains and the sufferings, were all just part of being alive, in this country of Australia. I needed to be strong and brave mentally, emotionally and physically; because I still wanted to see my family overseas. I had to kept on praying and hoping that, my nightmare situations here, won't be forever.

I wanted to tell my friend Daisy, but I did not have the courage, to tell her about my horrible ordeal. I was too ashamed, feeling embarrassed and helpless at the same time. I also didn't want to tell my family and relatives overseas, as I was worried they maybe will have heart attacks from it. So, each time I've spoken to my Mum on the phone and, when she would ask me how I was, I'd tell her I was fine and that nothing to worry about. But deep down, I wanted to share with her everything, so desperately.

One summer time; I was cleaning the air-conditioning. It was located at the top wall above the landline phone. When I opened the covering, I found a small black tape recorder inside. I pressed the rewind button and pressed play. I was shocked hearing my own voices, and all my conversations with my family overseas. I was confused, upset and really angry. So, when Preston came home from work, I had the courage to confront him. 'Why did you place this tape recorder inside the air-conditioning for? I've asked him.

'Because I wanted to know who you are talking to, maybe you have a boyfriend or a lover. I wanted to know everything. This is my house, I can put tape recorder, anything and everything around my house!!' He said loudly, pointing his finger at my face with his angry eyes. He was looking like a monster. He took his black tape recorder off, from my hands.

'It's not your business if I do get a boyfriend because I have no relationship and I am not married to you. Please, give me some space and privacy.' I begged him. I was too scared to fight with him more, maybe he will kill me at that very moment. I was living on the edge like an eggshell. I had to be very careful with my words towards Preston, because he would turn himself to be really angry and, could do and say something hurtful on top of his wrong deeds. My nightmares continued as usual. I was so very angry and just cried inside my room. I could not do anything, just living in fear and had no privacy at all. Living at Preston's house, my life was more than a nightmare, too stressful and I was feeling worthless. I do really deserve a little bit of respect and privacy as a human being.

I blamed myself, why I am here in this country. Sometimes I would walk to the pub, across the road from my job; to gamble my money. I've lost so much money and never win any cent, but I didn't care, because it was my outing. The Gym and gambling habits became my therapies, because I could not tell anyone about my nightmares and living in hell. It was very hard for me living with a nasty predator landlord.

Same thing, each time I came home, Preston would pressure me to tell him where I've been and he never believed me. In his twisted mind, he believed that I was seeing a boyfriend. It's always matter to him what was in his crazy mind, he wasn't the man that could easily agree or believe whatever others opinion or reasons. He was self-centred and always thinks that he was and will be in the right positions and everyone around him was at fault. So, it's pointless, a waste of time and energy for me to explain or to give him my reasons, why and where I have been. I sometimes I would just say, whatever.

One day I was changing my bed linen so I could wash it. When I lift the mattress up, I found the same little black tape recorder underneath, in between the two mattresses. I was going to break it into bits and pieces and, throw it in the bin as I was very upset and angry, but I was too scared maybe Preston will get mad and kill me. So, I've waited for Preston to get home because, I wanted to confront him again. As soon as he walked inside the house… 'Why did you put your tape recorder underneath my mattress?'

'Because I wanted to know if you are having sex with someone else. I wanted to know everything. Remember this is my house and I can do whatever I want! So, shut up!' Preston said.

OMG! I felt sick and disgusted, I said to him, 'But I am not your wife. I'm only a tenant. Where is my privacy?' Argh!!! F* you Preston. What the hell is this?

'Just shut up, well you!! It's your punishment because you are a woman. I hate women. And I can do whatever I want, because this is my house!!' Preston said and waving his finger at my face, with red eyes like monster.

He went really mad at me and raped me again as his usual punishment, but this time it was rough and very painful. I was feeling really angry and upset, but I could not fight with him because I still wanted to live, so I could still see my family overseas. It's so unfair to be treated like a piece of shit. I kept on blaming to myself for everything; for being stupid, for not having a knowledge about this country and for being so hopeless.

At the same time during my stay at Preston's house, he would take home alternately; different women into his room for overnight stay. He would introduce me to each one of them like for example; Babe, this is Rebecca, she is renting in one of my rooms. There were different women: Val, Evonne, Debra, Viv, Marianne and more with blonde and brown hairs. Sometimes they would laugh at me, after introducing me with his women, before heading to his room. I felt humiliated to be laughed at. But, it was good each time he has a woman in his house because he never nagged and touches me.

One weekend. 'Rebecca, I want you to come with me for lunch, at my parent's house today.' Preston suggested. I could not refuse because I didn't want him to get angry at me. So, I went with him in his car. He introduced me to his parents as a tenant paying $50 per week. I was feeling weird and uncomfortable, I could not say anything, I just felt like a robot. He also showed me where his dad's work at Newcastle area. Then when we arrived home... 'You are a psycho! Hahaha.' Preston calling me different name and laughed at me. I just ignored him.

Preston sometimes would yell at me for no reasons. He was unpredictable sometimes he would call me names: a twisted Reba, oi, nutsy, silly girl or stupid Asian girl. Sometimes he would point his finger at me, telling me to look at in his monster's eyes. I'm just getting used to it by now, coping his cruelties and bullying things.

I had enough, one day, I forced myself to get a boyfriend from work. I've invited a man called Allan into the house, for an overnight stay. My idea was, so, Preston will stop his sexual assault at me. The following day, when Allan went home, Preston got very angry at me.

'Don't you ever take a man inside your room and in this house ever again!!' Yelled Preston, waving and pointing with his finger at me. He was very angry at me.

'And why not?' I asked him. 'I am not your girlfriend or something.' What the F* it's not his business if I take a man in my room, as long as I paid my rent, clean his house and pay for my own food. It's not fair.

'Because you are only renting a room!! This is my house; and that you have no right to take a man in my house!! Do not make my home as a hotel. You must follow my house rules and regulations, woman!'

Then he raped me again on that day, he said that it was my punishment for having a man in my room. Again, I could not fight with him, because I still wanted to live so I could see my family overseas. I wanted to kill myself so many times, but I was worried for my family. I kept on blaming myself for everything. I hurt myself by making my finger bleed, sometimes I wouldn't eat at all. If I eat, I will make myself vomit. I hated myself, I hated my life and I hated the world around me. I even blamed and hated God too for everything.

On the following day, I've forced myself to ask Allan, if I could stay with him for a vacation, he agreed just for temporary. I only took one bag with me, leaving my other things at Preston's house. I have spoken to Preston that I was going for a vacation with Allan. He said it's okay, I can leave my things in my room. After two weeks of vacation, Allan suggested at me to go back at Preston's house, because we argued a lot. I had issues about sex and I didn't like being touch. So, I moved back again at Preston's house. He didn't touch me for a week. So, it was good.

One of my workmates called Leana invited me for dinner at her place around Toronto. Leana have met Preston before, it was one of her visits after work. Anyway, Leana suggested to take Preston with me at the dinner. I was going to tell her about his cruelties and bullying, but I was too embarrassed and ashamed. At Leana's house, I was so desperate to share about my nightmares to her, but I could not do it. I was just pretended to be a normal being as possible as I can be. Leana and her partner thought that I was Preston's girlfriend, which was really annoying for me. They had no idea what was going on behind closed doors. After dinner, Preston and I went home. All good, he did not touch me for a week, because he had a woman in the house. I wished there's always a woman or his girlfriend in his house so he could not touch me.

Preston continued his wrong doings; he raped me again for at least once a week as usual. He only stopped touching me if he had a woman in the house for overnight stay. He said that he can do whatever he like because it's his house and he made it clear to me, that I had no right to take a man or a boyfriend into his house because I was only a tenant. He should not be touching, or abusing me or sexually assaulting me, because I am not his girlfriend or in a relationship with him.

Many occasions on top of his sexual assaults, he would touch or squeezed my rear or bottom, or wrapped his arms around my chest, while I was busy at the kitchen; cooking or washing the dishes. Too f*ing annoying, uncomfortable and disgusting gestures. I didn't wear sexy clothing, as skimpy skirts, weren't my cup of tea at all. I've always wore long pants, with T-shirts or jumpers. Why wouldn't he behave like a gentle man, he was disrespectful, cruel and no good manners at all.

Living at Preston's house, I did not see any rainbow, it was all cloudy weather; even it was a sunny day. For me the sun was only shining just to dry my washing out at the clothes line. It was more than a life living with the nightmares and bad weathers all year round. My ambitions and goals to have a happy life was blurry and uncertain; it's all because of these maniac predators.

Finally, I found the Safe House phone numbers, the location was over at Lake Macquarie NSW. I've rang their phone numbers up, a staff called Melissa, answered the phone. I told her a bit of my nightmares and I requested a shelter for me. Melissa, advised me to start packing some of my things and, she promised me that she will be picking me up in an hour. Preston wasn't home at that time. I hurried up to pack some of my belongings. I was very worried, my whole nerves; body system was shakenly nervous and feeling sick in my stomach and, hoping that Melissa would turn up before Preston gets home.

After I packed my bags; I kept on checking out side through from the window. I was getting impatient; walking around in circle while waiting for Melissa. After an hour finally, a white van pulled over at the front of the house. Melissa got out and I did not wait for her to knock on the door. I opened it and started putting my bags out. I was only allowed to take two bags of my belongings with me, because she said that; they only had limited spaces. The safe house was only for an emergency accommodation for a maximum of three months, not for a long term. So, I've returned some of my belongings inside my room and hide it underneath of my desk.

At the Safe House, there were also some women or they would call them as residents, staying there. The residents came from the background of sexual assaults like mine and family domestic violence. Some of them were young women also with children. We all have our own bedrooms to sleep in, but we all had to share the bathroom, kitchen and entertainment facilities. There was a small playground area around the back, for children to play with: swings and slides. The food was free, all you have to do was to cook your own. Most of the food there, were all donated from grocery businesses around the Hunter. All the staff were nice and friendly. According to Melissa, this house was funded by the government. Some of their services was, to help as much as they could to all the residents. Helping them to look for private rentals or shelters within the full three months period. If for instance, there were no successes of gaining long term shelter, for the residents; the staff would then contact other facilities and transferred the residents to another safe house, around the Hunter Valley NSW. It depends also for the availability and their status. During my stay at this house, we had a craft day, just doing some painting, knitting and drawing. After four days at the refuge house, I rang up Preston, to asked him if I could pick up some of my things.

'Hi Preston, I would like to pick up some of my

things,' I asked him. 'because I needed them. I will get it in an hour or two.' Hopefully, he wouldn't interfere with my decisions. I wanted to stay in this safe house, so, they could help me to find a new place for me. This should be my opportunity to moved out from Preston's controlling, bullying and most of all his monstrous sexual assaults.

'Hello, Rebecca, where are you? I was worried about you. Please come back to my house; I'm so sorry for everything, I promise I will not touch you again, you can trust me and you do not have to pay for the rent if you like. I promise to you that if I touch you again, I will marry you. Trust me, I will not touch you again I promise, please.' Preston was begging me. 'Please come back here, I will pick you up. Where are you at?'

I was a bit feeling happy at that moment, because he made the promises that he will not touch me again. So, I said to him, 'I will go back, but I preferred to pay the $50 weekly rent as a tenant, just please leave me alone.' He agreed straight away and said, 'Okay. Done.'

So, I've spoken to Melissa and told her what Preston's promises; and that I will be going back at his house. Melissa agreed and respected my decisions. I thank her and to all the staff at the safe house for their kindness and generosity. All the staff was happy with the news so, Melissa dropped me back off at

Preston's house.

I had to make it clear with Preston, I told him, I preferred to pay my $50 weekly rent as a tenant, because I didn't want to have a relationship with him. He agreed. It was good he didn't touch me for two weeks. He continued his own things; taking home different women into the house for overnight stay as usual. Introducing me with his women, by saying I was his tenant.

One early morning, there was a knock on the door. When I opened it, it was a woman with blond hair. I haven't meet her before, so, I thought that maybe it's one of Preston's new woman. 'Hi, good morning. May I help you?' I greeted her.

'Is Preston, home?' She answered, with her pretty face, looking unhappy. Her hands on her hips like a smart and agitated girl, and at the same time, leaning her head a bit on one side. I mean, no smiley face.

'Yes, I think he is still asleep.' I said to her. 'Would you like to come in?' I was trying to be nice to the lady offering her to come inside the house. I wanted her to come inside the house, but I can't force her.

'Oh, no. Thanks. Could you please wake him up? And tell him that his girlfriend, Mona is outside.' She didn't come in, she preferred to stay and waited outside.

I went and knocked on Preston's door. 'knock, knock! Hey, Preston. There's a woman outside, she said that she is your girlfriend and, her name is Mona!' I went back to my room and lay down in bed, just relaxing for a bit. It was Sunday morning.

Five minutes later. I heard Preston and Mona; shouting at each other. What the f*ck... I got up and checked them out through from my glass window, hiding my head from the curtain of course. I didn't want them to see me. They were exchanging nasty words and unfamiliar vowels. When I say, unfamiliar vowels, I mean; nasty words that could hurt at someone's feelings.

'F* YOU!!!' Mona screamed at Preston. 'I KNEW YOU ARE CHEATING ON ME, THAT'S WHY YOU DIDN'T WANT ME TO COME OVER!!!' I could see Mona's face was really upset and angry. Her finger was waving and pointing at Preston. I don't blame her, Preston is a maniac.

'SHE IS ONLY F*CKING RENTING A ROOM IN MY HOUSE!!! SHE IS NOT MY F*CKING GIRLFRIEND!!! I AM NOT CHEATING ON YOU!!' Preston yelled back.

But they were standing face to face... and they were closed at each other... nearly touching their noses, why they had to yell and scream? I could see stickybeak neighbours from across the road, sticking their heads out from their windows and, some of them gathered around at their front yard and whispering at each other.

'F* YOU!! LIAR SCUM BAG!!' Mona fired back. Her left hand on her hips and her right hand waving on the air and sometimes at Preston's face. While her head leaning at her left side and her big eyes was full of rage.

'F* OFF!! IF YOU DON'T WANT TO LISTEN TO ME!!' Preston's wrinkled face was in a mess from yelling and screaming bad words. Yuk! His saliva went everywhere each time he yelled bad words. They were worse like Lion and Tiger fighting for one thing. 'Get out off my property, PISS OFF!!!'

I just covered my ears with pillows. I could not take those bad, nasty words and unfamiliar vowels. It's just too much for me. After another ten minutes of hearing their yelling and screaming. I heard the door shut loudly. Then Preston came inside my room and yelled at me.

'It's your fault that one of my girlfriends were jealous and angry at me!!' He was pointing and waving his finger at me. 'Next time, do not open the door, if it's a woman. Let me do it, is that clear? Look happened now! She broke up with me!'

'Yes, yes, Preston. I promise I won't open the door.' I got really scared for my life, Preston tormented me. My nightmares continued, he sexually assaulted me again. But I could not fight with him, because maybe he would kill me. I just kept on praying that one day Preston will leave me alone. I wanted to move out but I didn't know where to go. I didn't know about the law and where to get some help. I was too embarrassed to ring up the Safe House again. So, I just had to put up with all the nightmares. I was nearly losing hope and had a number of suicidal attempts. I wanted to end my life, but I was too worried for my family. If I had no family overseas, I could have ended my life now with a sharp knife in the kitchen.

One time, Preston demanded me to wash his work clothes because, he was feeling tired from work and wanted to go straight to bed. I had no choice, but to obeyed him. I didn't want him to get angry at me. I chucked all his dirty and smelly clothes into the washing machine, picking up his dirty underwear and, his smelly yucky pair of socks, with my fingertips and covering my nose at the same time. When it was done, I took the washing out and hang them on the clothes line at the backyard.

There was something fell down on the ground from one of his long pants. It was Preston's black leather wallet. I picked it up and had a looked at it inside, there were some money; two $10 notes and three $50 notes. There were also some receipts, his driver's licence and a photo of a woman. All wet. I was shaking and panicking and was so afraid of what would Preston do to me if he finds out about his wet wallet. F*ck.

I went inside the house, I used a towel to dry his wet wallet and the photo, I placed them on top of the kitchen bench. I could not think clearly, how could I dry his notes? At that moment, all I could think of was to iron the notes for a quick dry. I did it. OMG! All notes shrank from its' normal lengths. The sizes were small like toys money. I felt stupid and really worried. I placed the notes together with the other items on the kitchen bench.

When Preston woke up, he went to the kitchen. He saw his items and knew exactly what had happened. He still questioned me about his notes, asking me why it shrank like toys… I told him that I didn't know that his wallet was still inside his pants pocket and, the notes shrank, because I've ironed them for a quick dry.

Of course, he went mad at me; calling me different names: silly girl, stupid Asian girl… He told me, next time, to check all the pockets of his dirty clothing, before putting them inside the washing machine. So, these means I also had to do his laundry, on top of everything: cleaning his house, pay my weekly rent, bought my own food. I wasn't his partner or a housekeeper. I was a tenant. Why would he want me to do his laundry as well? Really? This is totally bizarre. As for me, it wasn't my responsibilities anymore to do everything for him. But, I could not argue with him, because I didn't want him to get mad at me.

Anyway, he punished me again, as usual… and

I preferred not to say it in details... because it was horrific. He punished me for my carelessness. According to him, I deserved to be punished and blamed me for everything, including for being a woman. He said that he hates all women, because his ex-wife cheated on him.

I'd get irritated; each time he would question me with unnecessary questions. Do I have to explain and let him know everything I do? Most times I didn't have the choice but to comply with his house rules and regulations. He would always get irritable if I went out without his knowledge.

One afternoon, I went to the kitchen I swallowed some bleach from underneath the kitchen sink. I went block out. Next thing I could remember, Preston was waking me up with his foot. I was laying on the tiled kitchen floor. I managed to get up and went straight to the toilet, I vomited out some awful taste. I was feeling hungry, but I had no appetite to eat anything. I didn't feel well for a few days.

I was depressed and unhappy, but I didn't want my family to know about my life in Australia. I just kept it to myself. I kept on praying to God, to keep me alive for the sake of my family overseas. *Is there any hope for a happy and better life for me?* I would ask to God.

One day, I was cleaning and dusting the cabinet shelves and noticed a weird looking thing that I haven't seen like it in my life. It was a thin double sided, glass; roughly three by four inches. Inside it in between the thin glasses; was discolouring red and nearly drying liquid. I held it up, trying to work it out and examined, what it was.

Suddenly I was frightened at Preston's quick action from behind me; he grabbed my arm and immediately took the glass off from my hands... and at the same time saying... 'Don't you dare touch it!!'

I was petrified. Preston held a grip on both of my arms, and telling me to sit down on the brown sofa. His eyes were turning red and a bit teary. I was too scared of my life, I wet my underwear, for a bit. I was like a little kid enduring the most painful punishment from a psychopath.

'Just sit there and don't move! I don't want you to say anything either. I want you to just look at me in my eyes and listen to me!' Preston demanded. He forced me to sit on the brown sofa and just to listen to him. 'I wanted to tell you something, I haven't had told about these things to anyone including my family.'

I tried my best to stay calm as possibly as I could. I didn't want to get into trouble. His eyes still red a sign of anger and bitterness. Sometimes his voices would rose in pitch. His melancholy wrinkled face, switches to different expressions; which made me feel uncomfortable. I was terrified of being forced to listen to his life stories and I was hoping he would not do anything to hurt me more. I didn't even notice if I was still blinking or breathing. I had to focused on him, it was his strict instructions. While he was talking, sometimes he would sit beside me, sometimes he would get up stood in front of me and sometimes he would walk about for a bit with his hands gesturing on the air. These was his tale…

'I was married to a beautiful blond woman at that time and was working at one of the Pathology Laboratories in NSW as a pathologist. One evening, I was feeling unwell and went home earlier than usual. When I arrived home, I caught my wife having sex with a male stranger, in our bed. I was f*ing pissed off and very angry, how dare my wife to cheat on me while I was working hard. My wife begged me not to kill his lover, so I let him go. I chucked her out the house as well and, told her not to come back. I screamed at her; calling her nasty names: bitch, slut and a pieced of f*ing shit. I filled for a divorce, went through our property settlements and bought this house. I went into a shit of depression, I could not cope and concentrate my job. I made lots of mistakes and more messed up; I mocked up blood samples and results for patients. The more I tried to focus and concentrate with my job, the more I made mistakes. So I got fired from work. I was on medications of anti-depressants. I needed a job, because I had mortgage to pay and a daughter to support. Luckily, I had a relative working as a senior officer at BHP and helped me out, to get a job there. And I am still working there up to this day. This glass thing, is one of the blood samples from the laboratories. I took it home, as a souvenir. After my ex-wife cheated on me, I had no plan and didn't want to get married again, as I have no trust to any f*ing bitch women anymore. I think all women are bitches and cheaters. I put all my anger and revenge on you, because you are a woman in my house… I have more confessions to make.'

OMG! F* you Preston! Why I had to cope all his revenges? If he thinks that all women were bitches and cheaters, I would like to think of Australians were predators because of this sicko and the other two rapists. I wish someone will rescue me and get me out from here. I wished I was a bird, so I could fly straight away now. He continued his talk…

'I have a spare key with your padlock, so I could get in and out into your room every single day. I went through everything you own. I have read all your notes and your diaries. I went through all your drawers and boxes of things. I like feeling, touching, sniffing and the smell of your clothes; whether they're clean or dirty. Sometimes I made myself cum, while I was in your room. I've checked your garbage bin daily for some clues and evidence for condoms, contraceptive pills and drugs; just in case. I just wanted to know everything about you and, what you were doing each day and your personal life. I wanted to know if you were having sex with another man. That's why I placed the tape recorder everywhere, near the phone and underneath your mattress. I was monitoring you daily. The idea of my tape recorder was; to record all your communications and movements around my house. Each day after work, I had to listen my tape recorder for some evidence of communications that you may had…until you'd finally found it. Matter of fact, I still have it and placed it somewhere that is hard to find and hopefully you won't find it… Please, do not hate me. You can call me a sicko man, but please do not hate me. I suffered depression since my divorced. I'm so sorry that I mistreated you, put all my blame and revenges on you. Please, I am so sorry.'

I would say, he did illegal search warrants, going through all my private stuff in my room and, on top of his cruelties. I was speechless, numb… this man is an asshole, a sex maniac, pervert, sick, psychopath and a dirty old shit. I was really angry, but I could not say a word. I handed him my keys, there's no point in locking my door. I could not describe for more of how I felt. I just went to my room and cry; wishing to have my family there beside me, to comfort me and to support me at that very moment. I wished my Mum would be here, right now to rescue me. I felt so alone and isolated in my whole life. His bizarre, creepy bad manners, bad behaviours, bullying had destroyed my self-worth and self-confidence. But the worse was his cruelties, the regular sexual assaults had affected my entire being. I was hurt and broken inside and out. Just wondering if there's God, if there is one…where is He? And why I had to get horrible and terrible punishments?

I did not choose to be living in this path, this was unexpected. My perspective about Australians had shift enormously with a shock. Why I had to tolerate with this psychopath for? An appalling realization had kicks in; my environment was extremely toxic, filled like with nasty Ammonia suffocating my nostrils. So desperately grasping for a bit of fresh air. The doors were all opened and yet, I could not flee. It was because of lacking of knowledge of what was available for me; resources for women's right, I had no idea and, the unknown I might be facing outside. I was too uncertain to go outside my box; too scared and worried as well, to tell my case or situations to the authorities. And if there wasn't not enough evidence for convictions; they might deport me. How could I tell and let the law believe me, that, Preston had put me into countless of situations were, my only option was to blink once, looked at the ceiling and waited for his terrifying assault to be over.

What I have done on this earth, to deserved and to be treated like a possession or a sex slave. It's completely shocking and horrific!

I was worried that, my life could never be healed in time. Well I ever get a happy life before I die? I am not sure, only God knows what will be my future. Do I have to blame God, for putting me into these situations, or all of these shits were just part of my challenges and trials. I am not sure if I could take more trials. My whole being system were so exhausted and damaged enough into killing myself, to end the pains and sufferings. But each time I attempted to kill myself, my Mum kept on appearing in my mind to stopped me to going ahead with it. So, I just had to leave my life in the hands with God, if He is listening.

Around 1995, I was invited to another birthday party and met a man called Sam. He was a gentle man and became my boyfriend. Finally, I moved out from Preston's house on the same year and stayed with Sam.

Sam and I got married around July 1997 and had two lovely children. My depression and my past affected my marriage. I feel weird each time my husband touches my body parts, especially on the sensitive private areas. I could not tell him about my past. I needed some spaces, personal healings and to sort out my life. So, after ten years of marriage, I filed for a divorce in 2006.

Chapter 4

The side effect of my traumas in life

I still have big trust issues in life up to this date 2017. I do not trust all employers, because of what had happened to me. I even advised my children not to get a job, because I didn't want them to suffer of what I went through, for over 20 years of pains and sufferings.

I still have nightmares and flashbacks most times. I often get triggered from TV news about crimes and sexual assaults. So, I avoided watching TV news for a while.

The three predators had clever ideas, (before they sexually assaulted me), by questioning me if I had family or relatives here in Australia. It was their motives to established my personal status or info and to make sure that I was alone, vulnerable and had no support what so ever.

I've seen the predators around shopping centres in separate occasions and, had panic attacks and flashbacks. So, I tried not to go to the certain places anymore. Because I don't want to see those predators, let alone to speak to them. Two of them had still the guts to wave and spoke to me, how dare they.

I do not trust: friends' husbands, males, strangers anymore. It'll take time for me to gain my trust again. I've always questions myself; why was those predators took advantage of me, was it because of my ethnicity, or national Asian background, and because I was alone and vulnerable in this country? I would think so, definitely my Asian background, being alone and vulnerable were the main factors.

I am still checking regularly my windows and doors, to make sure, they're locked at all times either I am home or not. My terrible and horrible ordeal had affected my whole entire life; I could not have a long-term relationship. Because, I still have issues when it comes to intimacy. I do not like being touch. I don't think I will ever get a partner in the future.

I don't think I will ever forgive these predators. For me, the three of them: the maniac employer, the selfish pretender and the psychopath landlord, I think of them all as a piece of the most disgusting and toxic ordure on earth.

I'd like to say, there wasn't any awesomeness for me between 1991 and 2016 that I have lived in

Australia. Except for having lovely children. Because as a result of my past, I'd been diagnosed and suffered with Extreme Depression, Severe Anxieties, OCD and PTSD.

I felt ashamed, embarrassed and dirty; I washed my hands a lot which made my hands super sensitive and suffered skin irritations. The GP prescribed and recommended a few different skin creams, but nothing was helping. Doctor said, the causes of skin disorders or irritations also was from too much stress, depression and unbalance life.

I still kept on blaming myself about what had happened to me. Even though the psychologists, social workers and counsellors; kept on advising me that it wasn't my fault at all. I still have trust issues; I can't go for a walk alone. I am hoping that one day, I will have enough courage to go for a walk and, hopefully it will be safe as well.

I still have no appetite to ate dim sims up to this date and, I banned can of coke in my life. As they're reminders from the maniac employer. I am still unemployed up to this date 2017, because of my rapist employer. In my head, all employers were predators. I'd rather be dead than to get a job.

Most times for over 20 years, each time I go for a drive for grocery or had appointments; I would normally make a u turn after over five minutes on the road. I had to get back home to check my door to make sure it was lock; it was part of having big trust issues. It was very annoying, a waste of time and energy for me.

I've experienced public humiliations and bullying because, I am still on a welfare benefit this year 2017. Some people would call me a bludger Asian girl or a pensioner pet. Some people would criticise me, they had no idea how it affected my life. I still did not tell to my friends about everything I went through my life; because I was worried they may judge me or won't understand or gossip about me.

I still have trust issues each time I put my washing out the clothes line, I kept on looking behind and over my shoulder. I had to hurry up to hang my washing, so I could get inside the house really quickly. For me, predators could be everywhere and could attack me at any time.

Some of my suicidal attempts to finish my life: many times, I would want to drive really fast and hit a big tree, so I won't survive. Many occasions also driving off the cliff around Newcastle, it would be a perfect way to die, because I could not swim. I've attempted to take a handful of rat poison, but each time I'm about to do it, my kids images kept on appearing in my head.

Most times when my children were at school, I just curled up like a ball inside my room, crying. It was really hard for me living with depression, I wished many times to be dead, but I was worried for my children; who will look after them.

Sometimes I would stare at a blank wall or spoke to an ironing board. Or some other times, I screamed on a pillow. I was getting nuts. I wanted some revenge and justice, but I didn't know how and I was feeling ashamed and embarrassed. When my children were home, I tried to focused on them.

Chapter 5

The Culture

Where I came from in the Philippines, rapes and sexual assaults had never been spoken. Because it's too embarrassing to mention about this topic, or subject and let alone to have experienced it in my life.

Around 2008, I've met a Filipino woman, Susannah over at the shopping centre. We introduced each other. Then shared our life experiences in Australia. She asked me what I do and told her that I am writing books and one of it was about my sexual assaults. Suddenly the atmosphere had changed. She asked me if I have a plan to publish my book with my sexual assault. I told her yes, definitely I would be, because, I wanted to share my own real-life stories to the world and maybe it could help others. Susannah became angry at me, she didn't want me to get my book publish with my sexual assault in it.

'Oh no. Please, don't you ever publish that book. Because it will give the bad reputations to all Filipino community around Australia. Your story will damage the Filipino community organisations and so on. It's a no, no, no thing to do. If you get it published, I don't want to know you.' Susannah warned and advised me.

What a stupid advised. This is for you Susannah, f*ck and screw the Philippine culture! No one and no-body could ever stop me in publishing my books, not even the priests or presidents or prime ministers etc. I wish she could read this book, so she will have the time to read this part. That's why I stopped writing my book for nearly ten years, because of her stupidity warnings and advises.

Around July 2015, I went back to the Philippines to visit my family and relatives, in my small province. Most houses had changed; from average houses or small nipa huts into big two stories houses. Good on them people, with their successes and achievements. But when I've spoken to a number of people about sexual assault topics, they tend to be ignoring it. They do not want to know about this subject or topic. They said because of the stigma, embarrassments and hypocrisy. Some of their opinion were something like, who would want to know about your rape experiences, I have no time to listen about it, it's too shameful to discuss about this topic. What the f*ck! That's why most victims like me, just kept quiet.

We had no voices and, if we do tell someone or to anyone, we get the blame for it. No one would believe to the victims or survivors.

I also encountered a Filipino lady in her 30s called Ana, around Manila City, we chatted about rapes. She too was also a victim from sexual assault. Her perpetrator was one of their neighbours; he sexually assaulted her for over three years. And when she told her parents; they disowned her and calling her a liar and some nasty hurtful words. So, she fled for the City and started a new life. I shared her also my very own stories which was in this book and she could not believe it, that it would happened to anyone overseas too. I wished her the best in life that a human being deserved. Ana now working as a singer in Japan. Good on you Ana. Wish you good luck for the future and I hope, we will see each other again.

Chapter 6

My messages to my rapists

I am so angry that you all get away with all your crimes. It's so unfair.

For the maniac employer

May you suffer panic attacks, guilts and shamed each time you see the bus stop shelters. May you feel the guilt and suffer severe migraines each time you see a red Holden commodore car and any red cars. May you shit yourself each time you go out for fishing. And, may you never have the appetite consuming dim sims and can of coke for at least 20 years.

For the selfish pretender (pretended to be a nice friend)

May you suffer the guilt, ashamed and panic attacks each time you see underwear and each time you enter every door including yours. And may you suffer the guilt and shamefulness and shit yourself each time you go to your bathroom for at least 20 years. And, shame on you for pretending to be nice and for betraying your dying wife.

For the psychopath landlord

May you feel all the guilt of cruelties each time you smoke and smell cigarettes. May you suffer panic attacks and shit yourself each time you open up your wallet. May you suffer Severe Anxieties each time you load and empty any garbage bin including yours for at least 20 years. And, may you suffer voiceless, extreme migraines and speech disorders each time you lock and unlock every door, including yours.

For these three predators

May all of you not see and notice the rainbow for at least 20 years. May all of you have those visions of all your crimes, each time you looked at the ceiling and each time you closed your eyes. May all of you suffer big trust issues and, won't have the confidence to go for a walk for at least 20 years.

May all of you feel the guilt and shamed each time you watch TV news about raped, sexual assaults and crimes. May all of you suffer sleeping deprivations, eating disorders, mental and physical issues for at least 20 years.

May your crimes haunt you all, for the rest of your lives, because you all deserved it. May you all suffer Extreme Depressions, Severe Anxieties, OCD and PTSD for at least 20 years also.

May all of you have nightmares of guilts, disgracefulness and f*ing shits each night. May all of you suffer, the discomforts, humiliations, very low self-esteem and worthless for at least 20 years.

May all of you have NO appetite for sex. And each time you think about sex, I hope it'll trigger the crimes that you all have done to me. May all of you feel disgusted, ashamed and guilty each time you hold your private thing, when doing business in the toilet.

May all of you get caught and get convicted. May all of you realised that, what you all have done to me was wrong. You all took advantaged of me, because I was alone and vulnerable in this country. Shame on you all. And may the three of you Rest in Hell and rot. All of you have no more power and control over me.

Chapter 7

The Healing Process

For the last nine years I have been seeing countless of counsellors: Psychiatrists, Psychologists, Social Workers, GP, school campus counsellors and telephone counselling with life line.

Up to this date, 2017, I am still having counselling with a psychologist, once a month. Each year I needed to see my GP to get a referral for a Mental Health Plan (MHP), so I could get ten sessions counselling with the psychologist.

I've attended Healing retreat at Heal for Life Foundation in 2014 and 2015. The facilitators were great and helpful and most of all, the place was so relaxing and comfortable. I thank you all who is working very hard to all the people who needed your assistance. And most importantly to Liz the CEO and founder of Heal for Life for her kindness and generosity for the community. Good on you Liz.

Doing crafts and photographs had helped me also with my healing process. It took my mind away from my past; these was one of my therapies for the last seven years. I will be producing a book of my craft work and photographs and will be publishing it next year.

Meditations and prayers had helped me as well, to keep me feeling calm and grounded. I do my meditations and prayers each early morning and, each night before going to bed. This regular regime, had helped me switch off my mind; from the outside chaotic world and my past. Very effective and lots of beneficial health and well-being.

Eating healthy food, like home cooking, less sugar and chemicals, had helped me to keep my health in balance. I do not drink soft drink or anything with artificial flavourings. My hands got better since 2015.

I had to be careful of what I would watch on TV. Gardening, cooking and the talent TV shows were okay with me. I like watching funny show or movies, because it helped my mind away from my past.

Writing or keeping a journal was one of my favourites; because each time I put pen to paper, it gives me a feeling of accomplishment. And, also this is to release and to expressed what was inside of my head. For me, writing is a similar thing like, having a personal counselling in your own time and privacy. Each time I do my writing, it feels really good.

Being in the present moment of the NOW, is a brilliant coping skills. It eliminates the past, not have to worry about the future and just focused with the present. Each time I got triggered from TV news, people outside and from the environment, I would just shift my mind or thought at the present. Nothing or no one could hurt me now. I am not the same vulnerable woman as over 20 years ago.

Chapter 8

Seeking Justice

In my case, it was too late to get justice because my incidents were over ten years ago, besides; the perpetrators lied to the police officers. They admitted it, but they said, they did it with consent. The predators were so clever; they lied so they could get away with their crimes.

One of the solicitors had given me advice to just keep going with my counselling sessions, to helped me heal my life. And hopefully all the nightmares will disappear.

If my case was under ten years old, there would have a chance to be receiving compensations from civil law. Since it happened over ten years ago, no chances for compo. For me, I wasn't interested in compo. I was more interested to get my rapists or predators get the conviction they deserved. But, the Law sucks. Because as soon as the predators said to the police officers, it was with consent; my case dropped to the ground, nothing, finished and being ignored. I just have to cope with it. That's why most rape victims, won't bother in reporting it.

One solicitor in Sydney had spoken to me around June 2017, he said if the rapist had been convicted, he could help me with my case to proceed it to the civil law and justice will be done. So, my book, is to tell the truth about what the f*ing rapists did to me. And, hopefully those rapists or predators will also suffer of all the pains and sufferings I had, for over 20 years.

Part of my healing journey was to get some justices that I deserved as a victim of crimes. And I didn't achieve it. I just have to continue my life journey, as for me, it is not the end of the world yet. I can still achieve wonderful things in life, I just have to live one day at a time and be in the present moment.

My messages to all victims, it's not the end of the world yet for you either. Be grateful that you are all survived from the ordeal you have faced. Don't give up life, you are all amazing for being brave. You are all beautiful spirit beings and keep smiling, as life is precious and wonderful at the end of pains and sufferings.

Chapter 9
Australian Statistics

Thanks for speaking out: Dr Bianca Fileborn, The Newcastle Herald Newspapers NSW Australia, dated May 08, 2017, by Damon Cronshaw. Twenty-four sex crimes occurred every week, in the Hunter last year. This included 11 incidents each week of aggravated rape, rape or assault with intent to rape.

Females aged 14 to 24 were most likely to experience sexual assault, expert say. The NSW Bureau of Crime Statistics and Research said, crime surveys show only about a third of victims report sexual assault.

Despite this, researchers say the number of reported sex offences is high in the Hunter and across NSW. "It's a horrible crime," a bureau minister for the prevention of domestic violence and sexual assault, Jenny Aitchison, said the culture of blaming victims must end. "We need to make sure we have education about respectful relationships at the earliest stage possible," Ms Aitchison said.

Sexual offences have risen 35 per cent in the Hunter over the past decade, crime data shows. Of the 1246 sexual offences in the Hunter last year, only 229 offenders faced charges. Bianca Fileborn, lecturer in criminology at University of NSW, said legislative changes had encouraged more cases of sexual assault to be reported to police.

Changing community attitudes and more stories being told had led more victims to report sex crimes, she said. Despite this, the National Community Attitude Survey showed a significant number of people remained "willing to excuse perpetrators and put the blame on victims."

"That does foster a culture where it's easier to sexual violence to occur or be enabled to occur," Dr Fileborn said. About 45 per cent of sex crimes in the Hunter were for the crime category of sexual assault (this includes aggravated rape, rape or assault with intent of rape). The remainder of offence were for a second category that includes indecent assault, act of indecency and other sexual offenses.

Antonia Quadara, the sexual violence program manager for the Australian Institute of Family Studies, said surveys showed about one in six women would experience sexual assault in their lifetime. The NSW Rape Crisis line is 1800 424 017.

I'd like to thank, Maitland MP Jenny Aitchison, the shadow minister for the prevention of domestic violence and sexual assault; for her time and for speaking out about her sexual assault. She speaks for the first time publicly about her own horrifying ordeal and calls for a community campaign on the issue.

The reporter or journalist of this article, Damon Cronshaw, will be contacting me very soon. So I could have my voice to get my story out as well. I am so thankful and grateful for Damon's time and for giving me the authorisations that I needed, upon for publication his article pages for my book.

Chapter 10

More facts and info

Myth 1

Only certain 'types' of girls or women get raped because they dress, look or act in a certain way. For example, they may be young, drink or take drugs, go to nightclubs, or hang out with guys they don't really know.

Fact 1

There is no such thing as a particular type of woman who gets sexually assaulted. Women of all ages, cultures, marital status and life experiences are assaulted. Many more assaults occur in a victim's home by someone the victim trusts, than by strangers.

Myth 2

Men can't control their sexual urges once they're sexually aroused.

Fact 2

Men can, and mostly do, take responsibility for their sexual behaviour. Sexual assault is not primarily about sex, it is an abuse of power and intimidation. Many offenders admit to planning the sexual assault ahead of time.

Myth 3

If it was rape, she would have fought back, screamed, or at least said no.

Fact 3

Offenders use many tactics such as power, physical strength, the element of surprise, threats, intimidation, drugging or humiliation of the person to silence their victims and ensure they don't fight back. They take away a woman's control of her body, her dignity, and reduce her to an object of sexual assault.

Myths shift responsibility away from the offender and onto the victim. They contribute to women remaining silent about their experience, blaming themselves or fearing others will blame them. *The offender is always responsible for sexual assault.*

What is Sexual Assault?

Sexual assault is an abuse of power and control by one person using sexual means over another person. It is a serious crime, whether it is committed by a stranger, or by someone you know. As an act of violence; it can cause injury to a person that may be physical and psychological. Every woman's experience is different, you may be very clear that you were raped or may feel confused about whether what happened to you was sexual assault.

Sexual assault is any behaviour of a sexual nature to which you have not agreed or consented. Sexual assault can take many forms, including:

Indecent Assault

Unwanted touching of another person's body. For example: kissing, fondling, touching breasts, bottom or genitals, being exposed to sexual acts or if under eighteen years of age exposure to pornographic material.

Rape or Sexual Intercourse Without Consent

Intercourse mean penetration of any part of a person's body by another person's body or by an object. This includes vaginal, anal, digital or oral penetration.

Sexual Acts Without Consent

The law recognises that consent to sexual acts must be freely given. A person is unable to consent when:

- Asleep, unconscious, or significantly affected by alcohol or other drugs
- Unable to understand what they are consenting to
- Surrendering from fear, threat, force or harm to themselves or someone else
- Pressured, forced or coerced into having sex

Even if the person doesn't protest or physically resist, it doesn't mean they agreed to the sexual activity.

Sexual Harassment

Unwanted verbal sexual comments or actions that cause embarrassment, fear or humiliation.

Chapter 11

Surrendering my life to God

For over 20 years, I hated my life, to the world, I blamed myself for everything including God. I had suffered extreme depression, severe anxieties, OCD and PTSD, as well as suicidal attempts for at least once a week when my children were at school. Each time I was depressed, feeling shit with my life, get triggered and had flashbacks from my terrible past; the voices in my head were saying…kill yourself, you are hopeless, worthless and dirty. My last attempt of killing myself was early this year 2017, my life went to the lowest point. But every time I was trying to end my life; the images of my precious children came into my head. And there were voices; saying do not do it, your children needed you. So, my children were the reasons why I am still alive today; I've chosen to live because of them.

One day, when my son was at school. I didn't know what to do with my miserable life, I was losing hope. I had enough. So I've had to surrender my whole life to God, the Divine Source within, I was on my knees on the floor... I had too many questions with God.

'Dear God, is there any hope for happiness? What is my purpose in this earth? Why you kept on saving my life? Starting from today; I am surrendering my whole life over to you God, I dedicate my life over to you God; all my thinking, all my saying and all my doing in your honour and glory, so I could live my life to the fullest. Please I needed your light, love and healings.'

On that very moment, some miracles just had happened. The voices changed, from suicidal of killing myself to living and loving life. These were the new voices.

'Life is too short and precious. To claim your real happiness is first of all you must forgive yourself from self-blaming and self-hurting, including to forgive those who had hurt you the most, your enemies. Forgive them to set yourself FREE, so they could no longer control and over power you. Freedom; so, you could just do what you love, focused with your health and wellbeing and so you could be well enough to care to your loved ones. Forgiveness is one key to real freedom and happiness. You must learn to

love yourself. Let unconditional love infill and unfold your holly heart. When there's unconditional love deep in your heart; hatred and revenge will disappear, including disharmony. So, let unconditional love overflow and enjoy life to the fullest.'

After that day, my life had changed completely. I shared about my new life with my psychologist, I told him about the miracles after surrendering my life to God. He had noticed it too, because during my counselling sessions in the past, my life was in a mess, not smiling at all, always had sadness, full of hatred and wanted revenge. He could see the difference now, I was looking happy and a different person.

Even my GP noticed it too. One day in March, 2017 I had an appointment with my GP. He said to me, you are looking happy now. Whatever you did, I want you to keep going, because it seems to be working.

I fully respect and accept all religions, all background and whoever they are as human beings in this world.

So, life is too short and too precious. To reclaim my life and to live healthily and happily, I must first of all forgive the unforgivable. It was the hardest thing to do for me to forgive those predators, who had hurt me deeply emotionally, mentally and physically. But I did it. So now I am a free woman, those predators could no longer control and over power me. I am starting a new life now. I am not silent anymore and I do not feel embarrassed or ashamed anymore because it wasn't my fault at all. That's why I get this book finished and published it so I could help others.

I draw my strength from God and I let him infill unconditional love, peace and healings into my holly heart and whole being. I let go my past and let God take over; as I have fully trust, belief and faith in Him. God never criticised me and He never judge me. He accepted me as one of His creations and most of all love me unconditionally of who I am, the same acceptance and love He give to all his creations.

I've chosen to follow the path towards God, the Divine Source within; to know Him and to let Him couch my life. God is my saviour, my mentor and my divine guidance. I surrender my whole life over to you God, the Divine Source within and I thank Him for everything.

Chapter 12

My life now

I am now focussing on how to get my life back, with God's divine guidance. I am writing fiction and non-fiction books for children and adults. I kept myself busy with my crafts, photographs and writing almost daily.

I don't think I'll get a partner in the future, because as I've mentioned in this book, that I still have big trust issues. Also, I do not like being touch.

I've enrolled in a number of courses at TAFE college and finished a few of it. I was going to continue to do my Diploma in Mental Health, because I wanted to be a counsellor so I could help others. But I could not continue because the smell of the cigarettes, students and teachers with similar voices and body features around and campuses triggered with my past.

I am still working out on how to forgive myself for self-blaming and self-harming. I'd like to be optimistic in all areas of whatever I wanted to do in life. I must extremely take care of my health, so would be healthy enough to care for my children.

I still do my daily meditations and prayers and, spend some time with my plants as part of my relaxations. I don't take anti-depressant anymore, because, I do not need it. Besides the tablets made me sluggish, feeling very tired and grumpy. I would prefer natural healings. As I do not like taking tablets or medications, I'm too scared of the side effect from it.

I thank Maitland Member of Parliament MP, Jenny Aitchison, also the New South Wales Australia, shadow minister for prevention of domestic violence and sexual assault; for her article from Newcastle Herald dated May 08, 2017. I would also like to thank Jenny and her secretary for taking the time to listened my own story, during my appointment and personal inquiries. I've informed them as well, that I would be willing and ready to speak out in public about sexual assault and to get onboard a community campaign on the issue. And she was happy with it.

I am not ashamed anymore about what had happened to me, because it wasn't my fault at all. If Filipino people will criticise or judge me, well it's their problem. I mean, screw their stupid culture.

I do volunteer work listening at people's life stories in face to face. I'd travel from Newcastle to Sydney by train, once a month. I'd shared my own life stories to the people and listen to theirs without criticisms or judgemental, and I respected at every individual's privacy and wellbeing. They shared their own life experiences; about rapes, depressions, toxic/domestic violence relationships, bad habits and homelessness. For them, it's a good feeling to have someone listening to them face to face; it's one way to releases their unheard voices and not being judge or criticised at and, most of all for free. Some people would share their own life experiences stories via Facebook private chat or emails.

Chapter 13

My purpose in speaking up

I am speaking up not for attention or publicity or sympathy. My purpose of this book is to share my true-life stories, have my voice out and hopefully to help others.

For the victims or survivors, out there just like me, you are not alone; please be brave and be strong. Because there is always hope while still breathing. Congratulate yourself that you have survived and are still alive today. Please stop self-blaming and self-harming, as it wasn't your fault. You didn't ask for it and you didn't give your consent to those predators or criminals.

It took me over 20 years to speak up because, I could no longer live in silence. I will not let my predators or rapist take the control or power over my life.

If you have been sexually assaulted in the past, please, report it straight away. Don't feel ashamed or embarrassed because, it wasn't your fault at all. And, take time to heal your life. Everyone is different. It took me over 20 years to slowly healing my life.

If you would like to share your life stories with me, or you would want to ask some questions about this subject or topic, you can email me: havingavoicenow@gmail.com

When you email me with your life stories, your details will be confidential. I will respect all your privacy and well-being. If I won't get my reply straight away, please be patient, I will reply back at you as soon as I can. It's up to you to share your own life experiences, it could help another victims or survivors.

This is really important for me to speak up. I'd like to recommend victims or survivors to seek some help or counselling, because there's always help & resources available. I'd like to tell them to take time to heal, everyone is different. It took me over 20 years, to start feeling normal and speaking up. Never gave up life; take extra care of yourselves, as life is fragile and precious. Look after yourselves so you will be well enough to look after or care to your kids or love ones. And I'd like to raise awareness of this issue and hopefully help other victims/survivors, in whatever they needed.

As for now; take care all and be happy, as life is too short. Remember, you are all have that especial being within you. You deserve love, respect and joy. Wish you all good luck, excellent health, successes and happiness.

Thank you to all my readers, keep smiling and live life to the fullest. God Bless and take good care of yourselves. I love you all.

Chapter 14

Tips after the sexual assault for the victims

For the Victim/survivor: Report it straight away to the police officer or authorities, the earlier you report the crime/s the better. So, the police officer or authorities could achieve the vital evidence they needed from you.

Mine: In my case, there were a number of reasons why I did not report it straight away. At that time, I was stupid and ignorant; I was only new in this country. I didn't know the women's right, I didn't have ideas where to get some help or resources I needed. My English sucks and I didn't have the courage and confidence to seek help. I was too scared and too embarrassed as well to report it. Besides, my rapists manipulated my head; that if I tell someone, no one will ever believe me anyway.

For the Victim/survivor: If for instance, you didn't report it straight away for some reasons. For example, you were too afraid or scared, you can take someone with you as a support person on your behalf. Ask a family member, or a trusted friend, or a social worker.

Mine: In my case, the reasons also why it took me many years before I reported it, because in the Philippines where I came from; rapes or sexual assaults has never been spoken. It's just too much and too embarrassing to talk about it. And, I could not report it alone. So, I took with me Ms Shirley Atkin, a Filipino lady social worker.

For the Victim/survivor: To save time and energy. I recommend to you, to type your statement and saved it in a USB device. This way the police officer, could just make a copy of it from your device, into their system. The detective or officer will thank you for it; for saving your time and their time.

Mine: That's what I have done with mine. I had my statement ready and saved it into my USB device. So, when Shirley and I arrived at the police station, all I had to do was to hand in my USB. The detective police officer, thank me for it. He said that in his over fifteen years career, this was the quickest reporting statement that he ever had. It saved us at least three hours, because each case could take for at least an hour. If you have no access with computer, ask or hire someone to do it for you.

For the Victim/survivor: Get some help. See your GP and request for a Mental Health Plan (MHP) referral and, take the MHP medical document to your chosen counsellor or social worker or psychologist; for your counselling sessions. You can request to see a female psychologist if you like, it's up to you. Whatever comfortable for you do it. You can ask at your GP's receptionist of where to get a psychologist or ask your GP for recommendations or alternatively, go onto websites and find your local psychologist.

Mine: Every year, I see my GP for my MHP, I then took it to the psychologist so I could have a counselling session, once a month. I still see a psychologist up to this date 2017.

For the Victim/survivor: Get in contact with Justice Victim Services (as it is called in Australia). Ring them and request to send you an application form for free counselling. They're services also is to help victims, recommendations to see approved counsellors. See their contact details on my resources page, they will help you also with your case to get some compo etc.

Mine: I had to fill out an application form and send to them. After two weeks, they send me a letter stating that my application was being approved to see a counsellor for free. I wasn't eligible for any compensations because my case was over ten years. But for victims as children, there's no time limit, they could still lodge applications for compo. You just need to contact Justice Victims Services for more info.

Chapter 15
NSW Government, Justice Victims Services

Support for primary victims

The Victims Support Scheme *(Victims Rights and Support Act 2013)*

Victims support

There are a number of ways that support is offered under the victims' support scheme. The type of support that can be offered depends on a number of factors, outlined below. If you have any questions about your eligibility you should contact Victims Services on 1800 633 063.

What support is available?

Apart from referral to other services, and depending upon your eligibility, there are four types of support available under Act. These are:

1. Counselling
2. Financial assistance for immediate needs
3. Financial assistance for economic loss
4. Recognition payment

"Primary victim"

In general, you are eligible to apply for all four support types if you are the victim of an act of violence that occurred in NSW and suffer some injury as a direct result of that act of violence (that is, a "primary victim").

You can also be considered a primary victim and be eligible to apply for all four types if you suffer an injury while trying to:

- prevent someone from committing an act of violence; or
- help or rescue someone against whom an act of violence is being committed; or
- arrest someone who is committing an act of violence.

Parent, step-parent and guardian

If you are a parent, step-parent or guardian who is caring for a child who is a primary victim (and who was under the age of 18 years at the time of the act of violence) you can apply for financial support to help you to take care of your child's needs.

"Secondary victim"

If you are injured as a result of witnessing an act of violence (that is, a "secondary victim"), you are eligible to apply for counselling support. To apply, use the Victims support scheme application for counselling.

1. Counselling

You are eligible to seek support in the form of counselling services under the Act. You may be entitled to counselling of up to 22 hours. The **Approved Counselling Services** provides free counselling to help address the trauma and psychological impact of the incident on you. It is an opportunity for clients to talk about their experience in confidence with a qualified, appropriately experienced professional counsellor.

2. Financial assistance for immediate needs

If you are the primary victim of an act of violence in NSW you are eligible to apply for support in relation to expenses that are necessary and urgently needed to secure your safety, health or wellbeing. The types of expenses that you might be able to claim are things like relocation expenses, changing locks, fitting alarms and screens, and urgent medical and dental treatment.

The expenses or treatment must also be a direct result of the act of violence and are available up to $5000.

3. Financial assistance for economic loss

Financial assistance is available to primary victims and a parent, or step-parent, or guardian of a child primary victim. Financial assistance is available to cover:

- Medical and dental expenses not covered under **financial assistance for immediate needs.**
- Expenses associated with criminal or coronial proceedings related to the act of violence, such as preparing victim impact statements and other justice related expenses. The legal fees of a legal practitioner are not included.

- Loss of earnings up to $20,000 (calculated at a prescribed rate)
- Up to $5000 for out-of-pocket expenses.

The maximum amount of financial assistance payable is $30,000 and must be considered a direct result of the act of violence.

A parent or guardian can also claim can also claim financial assistance, however the assistance needed must be in relation to the care of the child primary victim rather than your own personal expenses.

Only net expenses are payable. An award will only be made for expenses incurred after Medicare, health fund or other rebates have been deducted. If it appears that Medicare or other rebates are payable and no advice is received to the contrary, an estimated 75% will be deducted from the expenses claimed.

Note:

- Claims for **financial assistance for immediate needs** and/or **financial assistance for economic loss** need to be lodged no later than two years from the incident, or where the act of violence occurred whilst a child, with two years of turning 18 years of age.
- There is no time limit for victims of sexual assault if they were a child at the time the incident(s) occurred to claim for justice-related or out-of-pocket expenses.

- Before your claim is determined by the assessor you will need to provide receipts, invoices etc in support of any claim.

4. Recognition payment

This payment serves to acknowledge and recognise the violent crime committed upon the primary victim. A recognition payment may be made for the type of offence and ranges from $1500 to $10,000. Applications for a recognition payment must be made within two years unless the act of violence involved domestic violence, child abuse or sexual assault. Then they must be made with 10 years, or, if the victim was a child when the act of violence occurred, within 10 years after the day on which the child concerned turns 18 years.

- Claims for **recognition payments** need to be lodged no later than two years from the incident, or where the act of violence occurred whilst a child, within two years of turning 18 years of age.
- Claims for domestic violence, sexual assault and child abuse offences must be lodged with 10 years, or with 10 years of turning 18 for children.
- There is no time limit for victims of sexual assault if they were a child at the time the incident(s) occurred to claim the recognition payment.

Confidentiality and privacy

In general, the material in our possession is not released to other people. However, information may need to be made available to the offender if restitution action is taken to recover the money awarded. Your personal contact details will not be released. We may also be required to produce documents to a court where there is other legal action.

Victims Services is required to comply with the *Privacy and Personal Information Protection Act 1998 (NSW)* and the *Health Records and Information Privacy Act 2001 (NSW)*.

Charter of Victims Rights

In NSW there is Charter of Victims Rights to protect and promote your rights if you are a victim of crime. The charter applies to all NSW government departments. It also applies to any non-government agencies and contractors (excluding private legal officers and medical practitioners), funded by the State who provide support to victims. The Charter states how you should be treated and assisted if you are a victim of crime. The Charter is contained in the Victims Right and Support Act 2013. For more information about making a complaint, please contact **Victims Services** on **1800 633 063**.

Resources

You can Heal Your Life, by Louise L. Hay

Rape Victim Julie W. tells shocking story of being attack – YouTube, published on May, 2013

Rape Victim speaks out about attack – YouTube, published on June 14, 2012

Rape & Domestic Violence Services Australia (24hrs) – 1800 424 017 www.rape-dvservices.org.au

Suicide Call Back Services (24hrs) 1300 659 467 www.suicidecallbackservices.org.au

Resources

National Sexual Assault, Family & Domestic Violence Counselling Services (24hrs) 1800 737 732
www.1800respect.org.au

Lifeline telephone counselling (24hrs) 13 1114
www.lifelinehunter.org.au

Recovering from Adult Sexual Assault – A resource for women, their family and friends, NSW Health Education Centre Against Violence

The Newcastle Herald, Australian – May 08, 2017 by Damon Cronshaw

Legal Aid – 9219 5880

Law Access NSW – 1300 888 529

NSW Police Customer Assistance Unit Free call – 1800 622 571

Victims Compensation Tribunal (02) 8688 5511, Free call – 1800 633 063

Justice Victims Services – Justice Precinct Offices, Level 1, 160 Marsden Street, Parramatta NSW Australia. Enquiries and Support: 1800 633 063
www.victimssevices.justice.nsw.gove.au

Resources

Aboriginal Contact Line – 1800 019 123

Immigrant Women's Speakout – (02) 9635 8022

Immigrant Women's Health Service: Fairfield - (02) 9726 4044, Cabramatta – (02) 9726 1016

Community Relations Commission for a Multicultural NSW:

(02) 8255 6767, TTY (02) 8255 6758

Mental Health Information Services – 1300 794 991

National Disability Services Abuse & Neglect Hotline; Advice, advocacy & investigation guided by caller request. Free call – 1800 880 052, TTY (02) 1800 301 130 www.disabilityhotline.org

www.ingramcontent.com/pod-product-compliance
Lightning Source LLC
Chambersburg PA
CBHW021116080526
44587CB00010B/542